The Dentist

Alison Hawes
Illustrated by Shelagh McNicholas

Rigby

I went to the dentist.

"Can you look at my
dinosaur's teeth?" I asked.
"Yes," said the dentist.

The dentist looked at my
dinosaur's little teeth.

"The dinosaur can have
a little sticker,"
said the dentist.

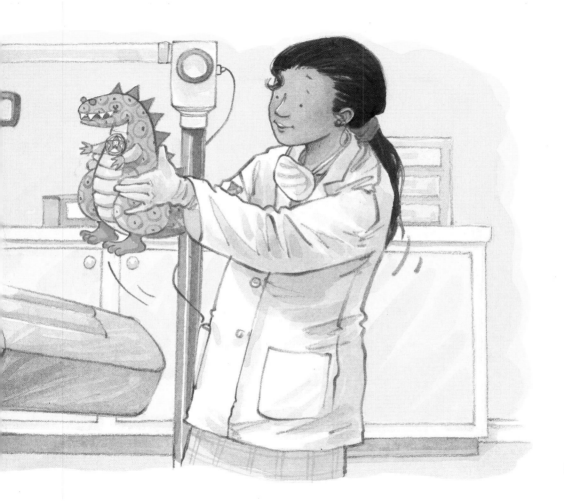

"Can you look at my teeth?"
I asked.
"Yes," said the dentist.

The dentist looked at my
big teeth.

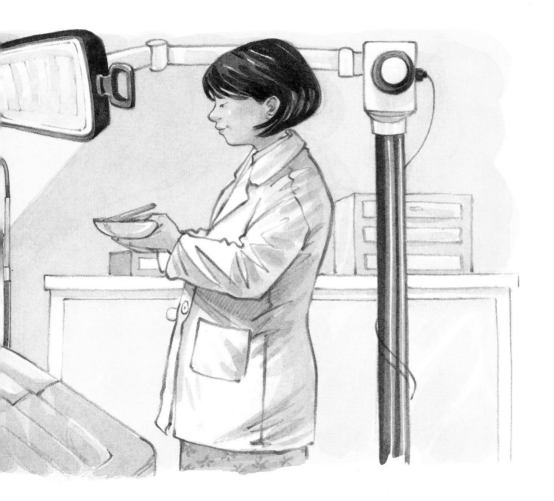

"Can I have a little sticker?"
I asked.
"No," said the dentist.

"You can have a **big** sticker!"